TOOLS for Children to Embrace Their Mental Health

Companion material to supplement
Butterflies in Me Anthology

PRACTITIONER AND FACILITATOR TOOLS

Written by Denisha Seals
in consultation with Katie Ladd, LISW, LCSW, LMHP

BOYS TOWN Press
Boys Town, Nebraska

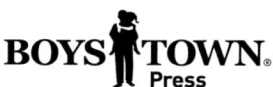

Tools for Children to Embrace Their Mental Health
Practitioner and Facilitator Tools
Text and Illustrations Copyright © 2022 by Father Flanagan's Boys' Home
ISBN: 978-1-944882-85-3

Published by the Boys Town Press
13603 Flanagan Blvd.
Boys Town, NE 68010

All rights reserved under International and Pan-American Copyright Conventions. Unless otherwise noted, no part of this book may be reproduced, stored in a retrieval system, or transmitted in any form or by any means, electronic, mechanical, photocopying, recording or otherwise, without express written permission of the publisher, except for brief quotations or critical reviews.

For a Boys Town Press catalog, call **1-800-282-6657**
or visit our website: **BoysTownPress.org**

Some pages in this guide are available for download so that they can be reproduced as needed.

ACCESS:

https://www.boystownpress.org/book-downloads

ENTER:

Your first and last names

Email address

Code: 944882bimfpt853

Check yes to receive emails to ensure your email link is received

Printed in the United States
10 9 8 7 6 5 4 3 2 1

Boys Town Press is the publishing division of Boys Town, a national organization serving children and families.

TABLE OF CONTENTS

Purpose of Toolkit		1
	Toolkit Contents	1
SECTION 1:	**Preparing to Facilitate Activities**	3
	Helpful Tips for Successful Group Leadership and Adult Facilitation	3
	Questions Children Might Ask about Mental Health Diagnoses	4
	Four Essential Group Rules to Share with Youth	5
	General Preparation and Supports for ANY Child	5
	Diagnosis-Specific Supports	6
SECTION 2:	**Children's Activities for Physical Body Awareness and Preparedness**	8
	Shake It Out	8
	The Mountain	9
	Move It!	10
	Breathe and Watch	11
	My Own Space	12

SECTION 3:	**Post-Story Group Discussion and Activities to Support Curiosity and Self-discovery**	**14**
	Discussion questions and starters	14
	Activity: Beanbag Toss	15
	Activity: Progressive Storytelling: Let's Create Part 2	16
	Activity: Guess My Gift	17
	Activity: All About Me	18
	Activity: Full Body Trace	19
	Activity: Obstacle Course	20
	Activity: Growing My Gift	21
	Activity: Teamwork Grow and Win	22
SECTION 4:	**Worksheets and Facilitator-Guided Activities to Locate and Celebrate Inner Gifts**	**23**
	Activity: My Butterfly's Emoji	24
	Activity: My Body Feels…	26
	Activity: How Does My Whole Self Feel?	29
	Activity: The Best Idea I've Ever Had	35
	Activity: My Favorite Things about Me	37
	Activity: My Favorite Place	39
	Activity: When I Found My Inner Gift	41
	Activity: All about Me	43
SECTION 5:	**Understanding the Mental Health Needs of the Characters**	**45**
	Character and Diagnostic Synopsis	45
	Diagnostic Information	47
	Reference and Resources	50

PURPOSE OF TOOLKIT

As an adult who works with children regularly, you're familiar with the general reality that they can be unpredictable, challenging, and create a lot of stress. Working with ANY child (individually, but especially in groups) is DIFFICULT at times. The sooner you accept this, the more you can grow your skills and become a more consistent, effective guide for children.

The youth you work with may never change or improve their behaviors and mindsets if you lack self-awareness about your own emotions, thoughts, preferences, and values and are unwilling to learn or try new approaches. Children act out what they see and what they are taught. As a teacher, caregiver, and role model, you create the social, emotional, and learning environment for kids. To help them thrive and make their environment less stressful and challenging, you must evolve personally and professionally. Whether working in schools or other youth-related programs, all adults must work collaboratively to support children.

This toolkit gives you permission to not have all the answers all the time and instead rely on self-reflection and your fellow colleagues. When you don't have 'perfect' answers or when situations don't 'perfectly' resolve, you may blame yourself or think you failed. The sooner you accept the reality that no one has all the answers and the sooner you practice self-compassion and self-forgiveness, the sooner you can approach children, especially those with behavioral or mental health challenges, with more confidence, compassion, patience, and understanding.

These pages contain activities that allow children to share their experiences, thoughts, and perspectives on the world. It also empowers you to create environments where children can celebrate their gifts and strengths.

Toolkit Contents

SECTION 1: Preparing to Facilitate Activities lays out several considerations when facilitating different types of activities with youth who have varied backgrounds, skill levels, ages, and needs. This section includes facilitation and group leadership tips, sample questions children may ask when learning about mental health diagnoses, guidance on facilitating activities, and specific considerations to help you facilitate activities with children who are managing their own mental health diagnoses.

SECTION 2: Children's Activities for Physical Body Awareness and Preparedness is designed for use with children prior to reading the stories in *Butterflies in Me: An Anthology Bringing Awareness to Mental Health*. These activities are especially necessary to help prepare children who have extra energy, a short attention span, trauma history, and/or other symptoms associated with challenging behaviors.

SECTION 3: Post-Story Activities to Support Curiosity and Self-Discovery includes discussion questions and activities to encourage children's exploration and curiosity after they have listened to or read one of the short stories. Children may see similarities with their own experiences or those of others in their lives. These activities can help open a safe dialogue and space for self-discovery.

SECTION 4: Worksheets and Facilitator-Guided Activities to Locate and Celebrate Inner Gifts is intended to help children discover things about themselves that they don't already know and then communicate those discoveries in ways that make sense to them and others. While these activities are useful for children of any age, younger children or those with lower developmental levels may need adult assistance.

SECTION 5: Understanding the Mental Health Needs of the Main Characters provides more insight into the mental health diagnoses being managed by the main characters in each story and includes diagnostic criteria from the American Psychological Association's *Diagnostic and Statistical Manual of Mental Disorders, 5th Edition: DSM-5*.

– SECTION 1 –

Preparing to Facilitate Activities

Helpful Tips for Successful Group Leadership and Adult Facilitation:

Important considerations to be aware of before doing any of these empowering activities:

- Stress is a direct barrier to learning. If children are stressed (visibly or not), they will not be able to glean the full benefits of an activity. So, it's important to provide the time and resources necessary to ensure children's physical/biological needs (restroom break, snack, water, rest, physical security, etc.) are addressed before starting any activity.

- *Butterflies in Me* highlights characters from various racial and cultural populations in the United States. Reading these stories requires awareness of one's own racial identity and culture, and an understanding that one's personal experiences are shaped by their culture of origin and their interactions with others whose backgrounds and identities are different.

- Be aware that these stories may resonate differently for each child or bring up personal memories that may be painful or emotional.

- We all strive to be competent, knowledgeable guides for our children. But it's okay to admit when we don't know something. Calmly saying, "I don't know. What do you think?" is a perfectly acceptable response when asked a question about a subjective experience or topic.

- Provide every child the opportunity to respectfully share their thoughts, feelings, and experiences. When this openness is encouraged, children gain confidence and learn how to express themselves appropriately. It also allows opportunities for perspective-taking and empathy because children will be exposed to the viewpoints, experiences, and attitudes of others.

Tools for Children to Embrace Their Mental Health

- When reading *Butterflies in Me* in a group setting, establish ground rules for the group. Rules can include:
    - We will keep everyone in this group safe.
    - Everyone will have a chance to talk, if they wish to do so.
    - We will let others finish speaking before talking.
    - When we disagree, we will disagree appropriately and respectfully.

Questions Children Might Ask about Mental Health Diagnoses:

It's hard to know exactly how children will respond to hearing or learning about mental health diagnoses, especially since children have their own individual life experiences, backgrounds, and supports. Below are a handful of common questions children may ask. Be prepared to address these and other similar questions. Space is provided to make additional notes.

- What's wrong with him/her/them?
- Why are they being so bad?
- Could I catch that from someone else? Is it contagious?
- Why are they so sad/mad/loud all the time?
- Why do they feel so worried?
- Why are they always too close and touching me/my stuff all the time?
- What did I do to make them act like that/do that?
- What do I do if they do something bad/dangerous?
- Is this my fault? Is this their fault?
- How do you fix it?
- Why won't they just stop acting like that?
- _____
- _____
- _____

2022 © Father Flanagan's Boys' Home

Practitioner and Facilitator Tools

Four Essential Group Rules to Share with Youth

1. Keep everyone (including yourself) safe. This means body, mind, and emotions.

2. One person talks at a time. This means when others are talking, your ears are trying their best to listen and understand.

3. We respect each other, even when we disagree.

4. We keep an open mind so that when we hear a new idea, we are curious and want to learn more.

General Preparation and Supports for ANY Child:

The following suggestions can help ensure successful, engaging facilitation with children.

- Some activities will be a great fit for some children at certain moments. Other children may not engage. If an activity does not engage a child, adaptations (such as movement or a sensory-based component) can be incorporated even if the child is not actively participating with the group.

- Children learn in the context of relationships. When possible, involve at least one leader/adult/parent the child is familiar with and trusts to increase success and reduce the likelihood of disruptive behavior.

- Help children destress before starting any structured activity by giving them a moment to engage in a fun, creative experience of their choosing (art, reading, games, music, movement, etc.).

Tools for Children to Embrace Their Mental Health

Diagnosis-Specific Supports:

Children who are living with and managing the following disorders may require some additional supports to complete certain activities. It's important to understand where they are on their own journey and make them feel safe.

- **Generalized Anxiety Disorder (GAD):** The most effective support for children with anxiety is a predictable, structured, and empowering environment. This can be done by having a visual or picture schedule available (in a well-trafficked spot) and reviewing it with children as needed. Let them check the schedule and cross off or remove tasks that have been completed. You also can get them more involved by allowing them to be "helpers" (gathering supplies, cleaning up, etc.) or assigning them specific jobs so they have a sense of purpose and connection to the larger group goals.

- **Attention Deficit Hyperactivity Disorder (ADHD):** Supporting children who struggle with ADHD means knowing their personalities and specific symptoms. Many children with this diagnosis tend to struggle with excess energy and unique sensory integration needs (touch, movement, etc.). Incorporating movement and/or sensory-activity breaks before, during, and/or after structured activities is essential. Difficulty maintaining focus for a sustained amount of time is also a common challenge. Depending on a child's age and developmental level, structured and seated activities should generally be limited to a maximum of 12 to 15 minutes. Children who struggle with ADHD often are easily bored if their hands/bodies are not engaged in some sort of physical or sensory input activity. Have a variety of fidgets available for children to use when waiting between activities or waiting for others to finish an activity. Some youth also benefit from having visual instructions, as it helps them organize the sequence of tasks they need to do. When verbalizing instructions, be patient and provide only one or two simple instructions at a time.

- **Adjustment Disorder (with anxiety, depression, conduct, or a mix of some/all):** Excess stress, anxiety, and/or depression affects children differently. But in general, youth struggling with one (or all) of these conditions tend to be unsure of themselves, impulsive or irritable, and may appear disengaged from what the rest of the group is doing. When children attempt to manage the symptoms associated with their mood imbalance, they often seek comfort, security, and stability. Having consistent, predictable routines for the whole group is essential for these youth. They also may avoid participating in any activity that involves sharing emotions because of feelings of shame or not wanting to be in the spotlight. Allow them to observe the group activity without forcing them to share their personal emotions or memories. Provide tools, such as emotion pictures or "break" cards, they can discreetly use to express their feelings or to communicate their need for a break when overwhelmed or stressed to the point of emotional dysregulation.

2022 © Father Flanagan's Boys' Home

- **Post-Traumatic Stress Disorder (PTSD):** When a child has experienced a traumatic incident (or multiple incidents that cause traumatic stress over time), their whole self — brain, body, thoughts, psyche, spirit, and personality — retains imprints of that trauma. Supporting children who are experiencing PTSD can be complicated and stressful. The core pillars of effective support for children with this diagnosis include self-awareness, patience, non-reactivity, consistency, and a fair amount of flexibility (as children with PTSD often experience intense and sudden symptoms at unexpected moments). To foster success, verbally explain the steps of an activity using simple, understandable instructions. For visual learners, have instructions or the steps of an activity on posters or visual aids to help them understand the sequence of tasks.

    Children also benefit from having a sense of control or purpose, so assign them one or two specific tasks, such as passing out materials or checking to see if everyone has what they need.

    A soothing, calming environment can prevent potential sensory triggers, too. Natural or soft lighting, a comfortable room temperature, and no strong scents, odors, or noises can give youth a sense of security. When possible, have other adults available who have experience with PTSD so children can have extra support navigating their feelings and managing their symptoms.

- **Autism Spectrum Disorder (ASD) and Pervasive Developmental Disorder (PDD):** Children with ASD or PDD often struggle to understand social cues, emotional expressions, and certain academic tasks. Communicating what they are thinking or feeling can be difficult, so having visual cues or supports (cards, pictures with labels, etc.) available can be extremely helpful. Children with these diagnoses also benefit from having visual schedules or illustrations that highlight an activity's steps in the order they need to be done. When verbalizing instructions, be patient and only communicate one or two simple directions at a time. It's also likely they will be extra sensitive (or less sensitive) to sensory integration, meaning any moderate to extreme sounds/visuals or touch can induce intense dysregulation because such external stimuli are distressing to them. Having this awareness and attempting to build an environment that respects an individual child's senses and personal space is key. Therefore, providing earmuff-style ear plugs, allowing children to stand rather than insisting they sit, and making other appropriate accommodations can lead to greater success.

    When possible, having additional assistance from trained, experienced, and patient adults (teachers, parents, etc.), who are comfortable providing support to children with ASD or PDD, can enhance the overall experience and lead to greater success for everyone.

– SECTION 2 –

Children's Activities for Physical Body Awareness and Preparedness

For Use BEFORE Reading Short Stories

These activities help prepare children who have extra energy, short attention spans, trauma histories, and other symptoms associated with challenging behaviors. The more enthusiastic, proactive, and engaging you can be, the more you can reduce disruptions. As a facilitator, you should demonstrate each step of an activity to show children how it looks and feels.

– ACTIVITY –
Shake It Out

> **This activity allows children to move their bodies and release excess energy in a structured and safe manner.**

Setup:

Ensure all children are spread out with enough space around them to freely swing and rotate their arms and legs.

STEP 1. Name a body part (foot, hand, leg, etc.) and ask everyone to do their best to shake out any extra energy (or sillies). Instruct youth to stay in place while they stretch or safely shake their bodies.

STEP 2. If appropriate for the size and age of the group, give each child an opportunity to pick a part of the body that everyone should move or shake.

– ACTIVITY –
The Mountain

> This activity encourages spatial and physical awareness using different body postures and balance exercises. You may need to provide extra support or adaptations for children who struggle with sensory integration and balance.

Setup:

Ensure each child has enough space to extend both arms out to the side.

STEP 1. Say the following aloud to the group:

> *Feel your feet touching the ground. Stomp your feet a few times then stop. What parts of your feet are pressing into the ground? Is there more weight in your toes or on your heels? See if you can spread out your toes and spread your weight evenly across your whole foot. If you're standing with more weight on the inside of your foot, try to shift your weight to the outside of the foot or vice versa. Feel yourself solidly rooted into the ground.*
>
> *Now think about your legs. How does each part of your leg feel? Make sure your knees aren't locked in place – bend or shake them a little bit and leave them slightly bent. Keep your shoulders loose. Hold your head up high and your neck straight, with chin tucked in just a little. Imagine someone is pulling your head upward using a string attached at the top center of your head. You are a tall, steady, STRONG mountain.*

STEP 2. Ask for volunteers to describe what it might feel like to be a mountain and if they were a mountain, what would their mountain be like (snowy, barren, green, filled with what type of animals, etc.).

Tools for Children to Embrace Their Mental Health

– ACTIVITY –
Move It!

> This activity helps children learn about and focus attention on their breath and how the body responds to focused breathing. This may be difficult for some children, particularly if they have PTSD, so participation should be voluntary. Those who choose to opt out should simply observe (sitting or standing) with their hands on their stomachs.

Materials Needed:

 1 small plush toy per child

Setup:

Instruct the group to form a circle, with everyone sitting or standing at least an arm's length apart. You also can allow children the option of sitting down or lying on their backs. Those who feel uncomfortable lying down should sit or assume a position that is comfortable and safe for them.

STEP 1. Demonstrate how to inhale deep and slow, then explain how deep breathing makes the stomach inflate like a balloon or bubble. You may even want to lie down and place a small toy on your stomach so kids can watch the toy rise and fall as you inhale and exhale. After your demonstration, let children practice deep breathing on their own. Give them the option of lying down with a toy on their stomachs.

Practitioner and Facilitator Tools

– ACTIVITY –
Breathe and Watch

> This activity uses visuals to help children focus their attention on deep breathing and how their bodies respond. For children who struggle with impulse control or may get overly excited about watching and blowing bubbles, extra adult supervision and guidance may be needed.

Materials Needed:

- 1 large container of bubble solution
- 1 bubble wand per child

Setup:

Instruct the group to form a circle, with everyone sitting or standing at least an arm's length apart. You also can allow children the option of lying on their backs. Those who feel uncomfortable lying down should sit or assume a position that is comfortable and safe for them.

STEP 1. Take a deep breath, inhaling slowly. Point out how your stomach expands like a balloon or bubble, then exhale slowly through your mouth, blowing into the bubble wand and solution. Explain how the bubbles you've created represent your breath.

STEP 2. After your demonstration, have everyone slowly exhale through their mouths and into their bubble wands and solution. Assist those who may not have the ability or motor skills required to do this exercise. Some may need additional assistance handling the bubble solution or their wands.

An alternative option, which is dependent on the weather, is to go outside if the temperature is at least 45 degrees Fahrenheit or less. The white cloud (water vapor) that forms when exhaling into the cold air is another way for kids to focus on and "see" their breaths.

Tools for Children to Embrace Their Mental Health

– ACTIVITY –
My Own Space

This activity is designed to help children see and understand how to have boundaries that are appropriate and healthy.

Materials Needed:

 1 Hula hoop or round rug per child

 Open floor space or area

Setup:

Place the hula hoops or rugs around the room. Make sure they are spaced far enough apart so everyone can swing their arms or move their bodies without touching others.

STEP 1. Begin by defining what personal space means. If appropriate, you can introduce the Boys Town Social Skill of **Setting Appropriate Boundaries** by describing its five behavioral steps:

Setting Appropriate Boundaries

1. Determine your relationship with the person.

2. Assess the "closeness" (or comfort level) that fits the relationship.

3. Create an imaginary line (a boundary) that represents your level of comfort. Boundaries can be physical, intellectual, and emotional.

4. If your boundary is being violated, take a step back and/or ask the person to give you space and respect your boundary.

5. If the person doesn't respect your boundary, remove yourself from the situation.

2022 © Father Flanagan's Boys' Home

Practitioner and Facilitator Tools

STEP 2. Instruct the youth to sit or stand inside their hula hoop or on their round rug. Say the following aloud to the group:

"If you are standing, press your feet firmly into the floor. If you are sitting, feel how securely your body is connected to the ground. Today, we are going to create a space of our own. Close your eyes and imagine you are breathing into every part of your body. Now look up, eyes open, and breathe into the space above your head. That space belongs to you. It is yours. Now look forward and exhale. Imagine your breath is creating a bubble that is as big or as small as you wish.

"Now turn around and exhale again. Imagine you're creating a bubble all around you. Look at the ground beneath your feet – that is your space, too. This is your place on earth, where you are safe. Imagine inviting others into your space – or maybe you don't want anyone in your space. It is your space, so you can do whatever you like."

STEP 3. Have the youth take a few more breaths, then ask for volunteers to share what they are feeling and whether or not they imagined asking others to come into their bubble.

— SECTION 3 —
Post-Story Group Discussion and Activities to Support Curiosity and Self-discovery

Discussion questions and starters:

Use the questions below to initiate group conversations and open discussions.

- What similarities do you share with the story's main character?
- What differences are there between you and the experiences of the main character?
- What does the main character really love?
- What gifts does the main character have?
- How do you think the main character feels when using their gifts or talents?
- How can their gifts help others?
- Are there other areas where the main character can grow and learn? What could help the main character meet their goals or dreams?
- What does the main character fear?
- Who is one of the helpers in this story? How do you know they are a helper?

Practitioner and Facilitator Tools

Post-Story Activities

These activities allow children to further identify and explore the larger themes and lessons in each story.

– ACTIVITY –
Beanbag Toss

Materials Needed:

 Beanbag or stuffed animal

Setup:

Ideal for small groups (no larger than six). Ask everyone to sit in a circle with you.

STEP 1. Gently toss or hand the bean bag or stuffed toy to someone. Ask the individual holding the bean bag/toy to share with the group a gift/talent they possess or to describe a gift/talent they see in someone else.

STEP 2. After sharing, have that youth gently toss or hand the bean bag/toy to another individual. Repeat until everyone has shared with the group at least once. If children are highly engaged, extend the activity for another round or two.

Tools for Children to Embrace Their Mental Health

– ACTIVITY –
Progressive Storytelling: Let's Create Part 2

Materials Needed:

 Whiteboard/Paper

 Markers/Pencils/Pens/Crayons

Setup:

Instruct the group to sit in a circle or straight line. After everyone is seated, say the following aloud:

> *"The last thing we read about [Character's Name] was _____. What happens next?"*

STEP 1. Ask for a volunteer or choose someone from the group to continue the character's story with a single phrase (three to five words said aloud).

STEP 2. Ask for a second volunteer or choose another person to add another phrase, building on what was previously said. Repeat until all the youth have contributed to the story at least twice. If children remain engaged and enthusiastic, go an extra round or two. Write down each child's contribution on the whiteboard or a sheet of paper.

STEP 3. After the final round, read the new group-generated story aloud or ask for volunteers to read the new story.

Practitioner and Facilitator Tools

– ACTIVITY –
Guess My Gift

Materials Needed:

- Play-Doh/Modeling clay (2 or more colors)
- Washable markers/Colored pencils
- Paper

Setup:

Ask everyone in the group to think about and identify their unique gifts or talents. Then have them depict one of their gifts/talents in a sculpture or drawing.

STEP 1. Ask youth to depict one of their gifts/talents in a sculpture or drawing using the materials provided. Give each child at least 15 minutes to make their art piece.

STEP 2. When everyone is finished, have the group guess what gift or talent is depicted in each sculpture or drawing.

If making art does not interest some or all of the youth, another option is to play a game of charades. Have each child act out (without using words) their gift/talent while giving the rest of the group one minute to guess what it is.

Tools for Children to Embrace Their Mental Health

– ACTIVITY –
All about Me

Materials Needed:

- Medium-sized or small rubber ball

Or

- Cardboard cube/octagon with flat sides

Setup:

Begin by writing the following questions all over the ball or cardboard cube/octagon (feel free to add your own "favorites"):

Favorite food?	_____
Favorite color?	_____
Favorite movie?	_____
Favorite animal?	_____
Favorite game?	_____
Favorite cartoon character?	_____
Favorite movie character?	_____
Favorite talent/skill?	_____
Favorite person?	_____
Funniest face?	_____
Favorite song?	_____

STEP 1. Ask everyone to sit or stand in a circle, then practice gently tossing and catching the ball or cube. Instruct everyone to catch it with two hands. Once everyone has had a chance to practice, begin the activity.

STEP 2. Toss the ball/cube to someone in the circle. The child who catches the ball/cube should answer the question under or closest to their right thumb. If the child is not comfortable answering that question, let them say "Pass" and toss the ball/cube to someone else.

STEP 3. Continue tossing the ball/cube around the circle until everyone has answered at least once. (With a large variety of questions, children should be comfortable answering at least one.)

2022 © Father Flanagan's Boys' Home

Practitioner and Facilitator Tools

– ACTIVITY –
Full Body Trace

Materials Needed:

- Butcher paper or large paper sheets
- Tape/Paper weights
- Washable markers/Crayons (multiple colors), per child

Setup:

Tape large sheets of paper to the floor or use paper weights to hold the corners in place. Each sheet should be large enough to accommodate a child's size. If necessary, tape multiple sheets together.

STEP 1. To ease children's anxiety, lie down on the butcher paper first and have a volunteer or another group leader trace around you. Once your body tracing is done, write or draw three gift/talents you have inside the outline of your body. Show the group your example and then have them do the activity.

STEP 2. Divide the group into pairs, if appropriate. Have each child lie down on paper while their partner carefully traces their outline.*

STEP 3. When the tracing is complete, each child should stand, step back and look at their outline.

STEP 4. Once everyone has their body outline, ask them to write or draw three gifts/talents and three emotions they have. Each gift and emotion should be written or drawn where the child thinks it "lives" in their body.

*Some children may not be comfortable or feel safe lying down while someone traces around them, especially if they are an abuse survivor or have PTSD. Give them the option of drawing their own body. Whether children work in pairs or independently, having extra adult supervision and support is helpful.

2022 © Father Flanagan's Boys' Home

Tools for Children to Embrace Their Mental Health

– ACTIVITY –
Obstacle Course

Materials Needed:

- Chalk
- Hula hoops
- Stopwatch (Optional)
- Small/Large cones
- String/Jump ropes

Setup:

Create an obstacle course (indoors or outdoors) with the group's input using plastic cones, chalk, rope, hoops, and other everyday items. Each obstacle should represent a past, current, or future barrier children have faced, are facing, or will face.

STEP 1. Let the youth label the obstacles so they reflect the challenges or hardships that resonate and have meaning to them. The obstacles are symbols of the things that prevent the youth from finding their inner butterflies and developing their unique gifts and talents.

STEP 2. Divide the group into teams or pairs, or let the youth participate individually.

STEP 3. If appropriate, you can time the teams or individuals to see who finishes the fastest. Be aware, however, that a timed competition may create anxiety or stress for some.

Practitioner and Facilitator Tools

– ACTIVITY –
Growing My Gift

Materials Needed:

- Tables (work stations)/Chairs
- Reusable plastic/paper cups or containers (one per child)
- Green floral or porous foam
- Jumbo popsicle sticks OR Large green pipe cleaners
- Confetti/Glitter
- Green and brown felt
- White/Blue construction paper/cardstock
- Washable markers
- Colored pencils
- Scissors
- Glue/Tape
- Balloon weights (optional)
- Paper punch (optional)
- Small beads (optional)
- Hot glue gun (optional)

Setup:

This is an exercise in creativity. Using the materials available, children will create a "growing plant" to symbolize their unique gifts.

STEP 1. On tables or work stations, layout the materials so each child has a container, foam block, felt, popsicle stick or pipe cleaner, construction paper, scissors, markers or crayons, and an adhesive (tape or glue). Show a finished "plant" so kids can see how the different parts of the plant are connected.

STEP 2. Instruct the youth to insert the popsicle stick or pipe cleaner into the foam. This is the plant's stem.

STEP 3. Have them cut leaf and flower shapes out of the felt or construction paper, and then glue or tape the cutouts to the stem. Kids can use markers and crayons to color the leaves and flowers.

STEP 4. Instruct the youth to add "rain droplets" to their plant to symbolize the nourishment their gifts need. Droplets can be made by inserting blue construction paper into a paper punch, using blue beads, glitter or confetti, or cutting and coloring circles out of white construction paper.

STEP 5. When the youth finish, have them place their plant inside the container. To make the plant sturdier, the foam can be attached to a balloon weight inside the container.

2022 © Father Flanagan's Boys' Home

Tools for Children to Embrace Their Mental Health

– ACTIVITY –
Teamwork Grow and Win

Materials Needed:

 Large, open space

 Balloon/Beach ball/Light feather/Bubble or Baloonie (strong, elastic bubble)

Setup:

This activity is intended to be done with the whole group but can be played individually or in teams if necessary.

STEP 1. Youth must tap or blow a balloon/ball/feather in the air and keep it floating as long as possible.

STEP 2. After a child taps or blows the object in the air, they should say one thing that can help others grow their gift or make their gift stronger.

STEP 3. When the balloon/ball/feather touches the ground or pops, pause the activity. Note how many touches occurred before the object fell or popped. (Having a designated "counter" makes this easier.)

STEP 4. Applaud and celebrate everyone's efforts and then resume the activity, with the goal of keeping the object in the air for an even longer period of time.

— SECTION 4 —

Worksheets and Facilitator-Guided Activities to Locate and Celebrate Inner Gifts

Some children may not enjoy worksheet activities, and that's okay. Many children simply learn and process experiences differently, and they prefer more hands-on, experiential activities. Please refer to Sections 2 and 3 for ideas and activities that will engage children who have more sensory-oriented learning styles.

The following worksheets are designed to increase children's self-awareness and decrease their self-shaming and self-criticisms.

Please note that answering the discussion questions should NEVER be forced. Some children may not feel safe or comfortable sharing their emotions or emotional experiences, so participation MUST always be VOLUNTARY.

 Worksheets are available for download.
See instructions on p. ii.

Tools for Children to Embrace Their Mental Health

– ACTIVITY –
My Butterfly's Emoji

Materials Needed:

 Pencils/Markers/Crayons (or any age-appropriate writing utensil)

My Butterfly's Emoji worksheet encourages self-reflection. Children will identify and choose an emoji or emojis that reflect how they are feeling at the moment. The chosen symbol(s) allow kids to communicate to others their internal emotions. Depending on a child's age or ability, you may need to demonstrate how to circle or color in an emoji. If no emoji perfectly captures how a child feels, give them the option of drawing one that better reflects their feelings. If children are willing, encourage them to also draw what causes them to have that feeling.

Post-Worksheet Completion Discussion Questions:

- Does anyone want to share their worksheet with the group?

- What made you feel this way?

- Is your feeling mixed with or connected to other feelings? If yes, can you draw a line between that feeling/emoji and other emojis?

- Do you know anyone else who has this feeling? Why do they feel that way?

- Is it possible to have more than one feeling at a time?

2022 © Father Flanagan's Boys' Home

Practitioner and Facilitator Tools

My Butterfly's Emoji

Instructions: Please circle or color the emoji or emojis that reflect how you feel inside right now. If none of the emojis reflect how you feel, draw your own.

Optional: Draw what made or makes you feel this way.

Tools for Children to Embrace Their Mental Health

– ACTIVITY –
My Body Feels...

Materials Needed:

 Red colored pencils/Markers/Crayons

 Green colored pencils/Markers/Crayons

 Yellow colored pencils/Markers/Crayons

Assorted colored pencils/Markers/Crayons

My Body Feels worksheet helps children get in touch with their emotions, examine their physical and emotional feelings and sensations, and understand how their feelings affect their energy.

Using the illustration of the human figure, youth will write or draw the various sensations or feelings they have right now and where those sensations are felt the most (chest, head, legs, etc.). If they are experiencing more than one emotion or feeling, youth should use different colors to differentiate them. Also, to illustrate their energy level, youth should color the human figure red, yellow, or green.

- Red to indicate slow/still energy
- Yellow to indicate medium/average energy
- Green to indicate fast/full energy

Some youth may feel like they have lots of energy in their head (green) but little energy in their legs (red) or vice versa, so it's okay to use more than one color. They also can mark their overall energy or "speed" level on the speedometer.

2022 © Father Flanagan's Boys' Home

Post-Worksheet Completion Discussion Questions:

- Who would like to share how their body is feeling today?

- Is this a new feeling? If not, when have you felt like this before?

- Do you have this feeling all over your body? If not, where in your body are you experiencing it?

- Is it possible to experience more than one feeling or type of feeling at a time?

- What gives your body more energy?

- What takes energy from your body or slows you down?

- Describe a time when your body felt 'just right' – not too fast and not too slow?

Tools for Children to Embrace Their Mental Health

My Body Feels...

Instructions: Read the paragraph below and then answer the questions to the best of your ability. When you finish, use the illustration of the human body to write or draw how you feel right now. Use the speedometer illustration to mark how much energy (or speed) you have today.

Your body can feel many things but understanding or knowing what those feelings are can be tricky. To get in touch with your feelings, answer these questions:

1. Does my body feel **fast, medium,** or **slow** right now? (Circle one)

2. Does my body hurt anywhere? _____
   _____
   _____

3. Does my body feel something else or want something else right now? _____
   _____
   _____
   _____
   _____

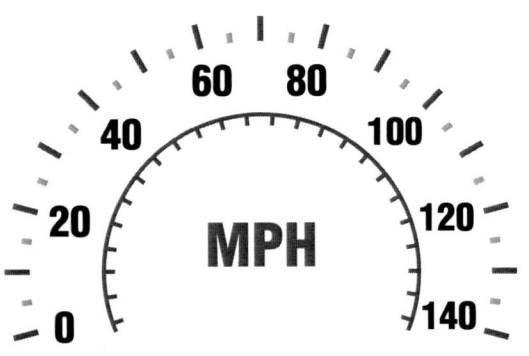

2022 © Father Flanagan's Boys' Home

Practitioner and Facilitator Tools

– ACTIVITY –
How Does My Whole Self Feel?

Materials Needed:

- Pencils/Markers/Crayons

How Does My Whole Self Feel? worksheet is a five-page questionnaire that helps children get in touch with their internal experiences and communicate those experiences to others through writing and drawing.

Post-Worksheet Completion Discussion Questions:

- Who would like to describe how their whole self feels right now?

- Is this a new feeling for you? If not, when have you felt like this before?

- Do you think certain emotions "live" in specific parts of your body?

- Is it possible to experience more than one feeling or type of feeling at a time?

- What's it like when your whole self experiences more than one feeling at a time?

Tools for Children to Embrace Their Mental Health

How Does My Whole Self Feel?

Instructions: Complete each sentence by writing in the space provided, then draw your "whole self" picture.

I feel happy when _____ .

When my body feels happy, it _____ .

When I feel happy, I usually _____ .

**HERE'S A PICTURE OF WHAT MY HAPPY
WHOLE SELF LOOKS LIKE:**

PAGE 1 – HAPPY

2022 © Father Flanagan's Boys' Home

Practitioner and Facilitator Tools

How Does My Whole Self Feel?

Instructions: Complete each sentence by writing in the space provided, then draw your "whole self" picture.

I feel mad when _____.

When my body feels mad, it _____.

When I feel mad, I usually _____.

HERE'S A PICTURE OF WHAT MY MAD WHOLE SELF LOOKS LIKE:

PAGE 2 – MAD

2022 © Father Flanagan's Boys' Home

Tools for Children to Embrace Their Mental Health

How Does My Whole Self Feel?

Instructions: Complete each sentence by writing in the space provided, then draw your "whole self" picture.

I feel confused when _____ .

When my body feels confused, it _____ .

When I feel confused, I usually _____ .

HERE'S A PICTURE OF WHAT MY CONFUSED WHOLE SELF LOOKS LIKE:

PAGE 3 – CONFUSED

Practitioner and Facilitator Tools

How Does My Whole Self Feel?

Instructions: Complete each sentence by writing in the space provided, then draw your "whole self" picture.

I feel scared or worried when _____.

When my body feels scared or worried, it _____.

When I feel scared or worried, I usually_____.

HERE'S A PICTURE OF WHAT MY SCARED/WORRIED WHOLE SELF LOOKS LIKE:

PAGE 4 – SCARED/WORRIED

2022 © Father Flanagan's Boys' Home

Tools for Children to Embrace Their Mental Health

How Does My Whole Self Feel?

Instructions: Complete each sentence by writing in the space provided, then draw your "whole self" picture.

I feel proud of myself when _____ .

When my body feels proud, it _____ .

When I feel proud, I usually _____ .

HERE'S A PICTURE OF WHAT MY PROUD WHOLE SELF LOOKS LIKE:

PAGE 5 – PROUD

2022 © Father Flanagan's Boys' Home

Practitioner and Facilitator Tools

– ACTIVITY –
The Best Idea I've Ever Had

Materials Needed:

- Pencils/Markers/Crayons

The Best Idea I've Ever Had worksheet invites children to explain and share an idea that made them feel proud and excited. Children are naturally curious, but sometimes their curiosity is discouraged. Providing more opportunities to engage their curiosity and explore ideas can improve their cognitive skills, social and emotional awareness, independent problem-solving skills, and imagination. Using words and drawings, kids will freely express their ideas.

Post-Worksheet Completion Discussion Questions:

- Who would like to share details about the best idea they ever had?

- How did you feel when you came up with this idea?

- Was that a new feeling for you? If not, when have you felt like that before?

- Did you have mixed or many feelings when you came up with the idea?

- Is it possible to experience more than one feeling or type of feeling at a time?

- What kind of ideas do you think you'll come up with in the future?

2022 © Father Flanagan's Boys' Home

Tools for Children to Embrace Their Mental Health

The Best Idea I've Ever Had

Instructions: Read the sentence below and then use the space provided to draw a picture of your BEST IDEA EVER.

THIS ONE TIME, I HAD THE BEST IDEA EVER. HERE IS A PICTURE OF IT.

Practitioner and Facilitator Tools

– ACTIVITY –
My Favorite Things about Me

Materials Needed:

 Pencils/Markers/Crayons

My Favorite Things About Me worksheet helps children build their self-awareness by identifying and exploring the things they like about themselves. By finding joy in what makes them who they are, children can raise their self-esteem, gain confidence, and improve their social and emotional skills.

Post-Worksheet Completion Discussion Questions:

- Did you find out something new about yourself while doing this activity? If yes, what?

- How did you feel when you answered the "thing you like best about yourself" question?

- Was that a new feeling for you? If not, when have you felt like that before?

- Before doing this activity, had you ever taken time to reflect on what you like about yourself?

- Are there more things you like about yourself? What are they?

- What do you want your future self to be like?

2022 © Father Flanagan's Boys' Home

Tools for Children to Embrace Their Mental Health

My Favorite Things about Me

Instructions: Complete the following sentences in the space provided.

There are a lot of great things about me. Here are some of my favorites.

The thing I like best about myself is _____

_____.

My body is awesome because it can _____

_____.

My personality is really wonderful because_____

_____.

I'm a great friend because_____

_____.

The thing I am most proud of is _____

_____.

2022 © Father Flanagan's Boys' Home

Practitioner and Facilitator Tools

– ACTIVITY –
My Favorite Place

Materials Needed:

 Pencils/Markers/Crayons

My Favorite Place worksheet asks children to describe the place where they feel at peace, safe, and can be the best version of themselves. For many children, certain locations can trigger specific emotions, be a reminder of past sensory and physical experiences, and hold other memories. Being able to describe the place or location that gives them a sense of security, safety, and peace helps children better understand the type of environment they need to successfully self-regulate (emotionally, behaviorally, and psychologically).

Post-Worksheet Completion Discussion Questions:

- Who would like to describe their favorite place?

- How did you feel when thinking about your favorite place?

- Was that a new feeling for you? If not, when have you felt like that before?

- Do you wish you could be in your favorite place all the time? Why?

- What other things do you like about your favorite place?

- Do you think it will always be your favorite place? If not, why?

Tools for Children to Embrace Their Mental Health

Favorite Place

Instructions: Complete each sentence by writing in the space provided, then draw a picture of your favorite place.

Everyone has a favorite place. This place can be ANYWHERE.

My favorite place is _____.

I found this place when _____.

It reminds me of _____.

The best thing about this place is _____.

When I am in this place, I feel _____.

I DREW A PICTURE SO YOU CAN SEE WHAT IT LOOKS LIKE.

Practitioner and Facilitator Tools

– ACTIVITY –
When I Found My Inner Gift

Materials Needed:

- Pencils/Markers/Crayons

When I Found My Inner Gift worksheet requires children to have a degree of self-awareness. Some children may not have discovered their inner gift or may not understand how to explain such an abstract concept in a concrete way. Therefore, you should ask and discuss the Pre-Worksheet Context Questions. The questions will encourage abstract thinking and help children get into the right mindset for this activity.

In addition to the pre-worksheet questions, you will need to define what "inner gifts" mean. It can be defined as "a special talent or way of doing something that is unique to you and makes you special."

Pre-Worksheet Context Questions to Encourage Abstract Thinking:

- What does having a 'talent' mean?
- What does 'special' mean?
- Who is your favorite superhero? What special superpower would you like to have?

Post-Worksheet Completion Discussion Questions:

- How did you feel when you discovered your inner gift?
- Was that a new feeling for you? If not, when have you felt like that before?
- In your journey to find your inner gift, what problems or challenges did you experience?
- Do you share your inner gift with others? If so, how?
- Do you think you have more inner gifts? If yes, what might they be?

Tools for Children to Embrace Their Mental Health

When I Found My Inner Gift

Instructions: Complete each sentence by writing in the space provided, then draw a picture of your inner gift.

Finding my inner gift wasn't easy. It took some work and determination. When I found my gift, the first thing I said to myself (or someone else) was _____ _____.

My gift reminds me of _____.

It makes me feel really _____.

MY GIFT LOOKS LIKE THIS:

2022 © Father Flanagan's Boys' Home

Practitioner and Facilitator Tools

– ACTIVITY –
All about Me

Materials Needed:

 Pencils/Markers/Crayons

All about Me worksheet empowers children by letting them choose how they want others to know them. This activity is a great way for you to learn more about the children in your group and for them to learn about each other. As mentioned in the introduction to Section 4, please remember that sharing with the group or answering discussion questions must never be forced. Some children may not feel safe or comfortable revealing personal feelings or experiences, so participation should always be voluntary.

Post-Worksheet Completion Discussion Questions:

- Did this activity change how you think about yourself? Did your answers surprise you?

- What question was the most interesting to you?

- How did answering that question (the one you consider the most interesting) make you feel?

- Was that a new feeling for you? If not, when have you felt like that before?

- What question would you add to this activity?

- What question would you take out of this activity?

Tools for Children to Embrace Their Mental Health

All about Me

Instructions: Complete each sentence by writing in the space provided.

I dream of _____ .

I worry that _____ .

An important thing to know about me is _____
_____ .

I believe _____ .

Sometimes it's tough to _____
_____ .

I used to _____ .

I feel like _____ .

It's hard to _____ .

I don't like_____ .

Sometimes I need help with _____ .

I feel most comfortable when _____ .

I feel most uncomfortable when _____ .

I'm in the "Zone" when _____ .

The most important thing to me is _____ .

– SECTION 5 –

Understanding the Mental Health Needs of the Characters

Character and Diagnostic Synopsis

The main character in each Butterfly story is listed below along with the mental health issue they are managing. The descriptions of each diagnosis will help you better understand and relate to the experiences and feelings of children and their caregivers who are living with similar diagnoses. For more in-depth information about a diagnosis, refer to the Diagnostic Information on pages 47-49.

Javier Sanchez
14 years old
Post Traumatic Stress Disorder (PTSD)

PTSD is one of the more complex diagnoses in adults and children, as it manifests differently depending on the individual and their exposure to traumatic stress. PTSD means that a person has experienced something that created a sense of powerlessness and/or fear that they or someone else would be seriously injured or killed. This is called traumatic stress exposure. Traumatic stress exposure can affect not only mental health, but physical health and one's susceptibility to having future chronic health problems. For most children, PTSD can appear as anger management struggles (including physical aggression), risky or dangerous behaviors, inappropriate social skills or extreme rudeness, lack of empathy for others, excessive energy, extreme mood swings, an inability to pay attention, forgetfulness, intrusive flashbacks, bedtime avoidance and anxiety, nightmares and sleep disruptions, exaggerated startle responses or extremely watchful/paranoid, and hypervigilance.

2022 © Father Flanagan's Boys' Home

Tools for Children to Embrace Their Mental Health

Kenya Olew
7 years old
Generalized Anxiety Disorder (GAD)

GAD means a person experiences persistent or exaggerated feelings of worry or anxiety that can interfere with daily activities, including social interactions. For children, GAD can cause them to repeatedly ask the same questions, have separation anxiety, feel sick, scared or tired, lose sleep, and be more fearful around others.

Abbas Kidjo
9 years old
Attention Deficit Hyperactivity Disorder (ADHD)

ADHD means a person often has difficulty keeping their focus and staying organized. Other symptoms can include talking a lot, interrupting others, excessive restlessness, difficulty multitasking, impulsiveness, and problems following through and completing tasks. Children with ADHD also can experience sudden mood swings, be short-tempered, engage in risky behaviors, struggle with planning, and have poor time-management skills. They may also have learning disabilities or other delays.

LuLu Whitebear
12 years old
Adjustment Disorder, Unspecified (Situational, Grief Induced)

An Adjustment Disorder is generally diagnosed in children (but can be diagnosed in adults) and means they struggle due to a life change or increased stress. It can be triggered by the death of a loved one, a move, divorce, a new baby entering the family, and other stressful triggers. Adjustment disorders can be associated with depression, anxiety, anger/aggressive behaviors, or a combination of each. In LuLu's story, she is extremely sad and lonely because her beloved Grandma died. Many children under the age of 5 struggle to understand the concept of death, however LuLu is 11. She understands her grandmother is gone and not coming back. Children with Adjustment Disorder feel much more intense emotions more frequently. They might cry or tear up suddenly or unexpectedly, be irritable or crabby, have little energy, have difficulty sleeping, and may not enjoy previously enjoyable activities or situations.

2022 © Father Flanagan's Boys' Home

Diagnostic Information

Diagnostic Criteria Clinical Definitions, from the American Psychological Association's Diagnostic and Statistical Manual of Mental Disorders, 5th Edition: DSM-5 (APA, 2013).

Post-Traumatic Stress Disorder (PTSD)

PTSD is diagnosed by a clinician when a person has experienced or witnessed a shocking or disturbing event that involves death, threatened death, actual or threatened serious injury, and sexual violence or threatened sexual violation. To be diagnosed with PTSD, and individual must fulfill the following criteria by a physician or a licensed mental health professional:

Criterion A: Stressor (exposure to at least one traumatic event)

Criterion B: Intrusive symptoms (memories, thoughts, involuntary bodily reactions)

Criterion C: Avoidance (effortful avoidance of trauma-related stimuli)

Criterion D: Negative changes in thought and/or mood (experiencing two or more of the following: inability to recall key parts of the event; persistent and distorted negative beliefs about self/others [e.g., I am unlovable. The world is an evil place.]; pervasive negative emotional state; loss of formerly enjoyed interests; feeling alienated or detached from others; and persistent inability to experience positive emotions).

Criterion E: Alterations in arousal and reactivity (experiencing two or more of the following: difficulty concentrating, hypervigilant, heightened startle response, impulsive or self-destructive behavior, irritability or aggression, and problems sleeping).

Criterion F: Duration (above symptoms last for a month or more).

Criterion G: Functional significance (symptoms create distress and/or interfere with school, family, friendships, work, etc.).

Criterion H: Exclusion (symptoms not due to a medical condition, currently prescribed medication, or some form of substance use).

Generalized Anxiety Disorder (GAD)

Generalized Anxiety Disorder is diagnosed by a clinician when a person appears to experience and reports to have the following symptoms for at least six months: worry that is difficult to control (and takes up a significant portion of waking hours); worry that shifts from one topic to another; edginess; restlessness; more fatigued than usual; impaired concentration; more irritable than usual; and difficulty sleeping.

These symptoms must be unrelated to any other medical conditions and cannot be explained by a different mental disorder or by the effects of substance use, including prescriptions, alcohol, or recreational drugs.

Attention Deficit Hyperactivity Disorder (ADHD)

ADHD is diagnosed by a clinician when a person appears and reports to have a persistent pattern of inattention and/or hyperactivity-impulsivity.

Inattention can include the following symptoms: often distracted; often struggles to hold attention or focus on tasks or play activities; often does not seem to listen when spoken to directly; often struggles to follow through on instructions; often struggles with organizing tasks and activities; and often loses things necessary to complete a task or activity.

Hyperactivity-impulsivity symptoms can include: often fidgets with or taps hands or feet, or squirms in seat; often leaves seat when remaining seated is expected; often talks excessively; often has trouble waiting their turn; often interrupts/intrudes on others; and blurts out an answer before a question has been completed.

These symptoms must be unrelated to any other medical conditions and cannot be explained by a different mental disorder or by the effects of substance use, including prescriptions, alcohol, or recreational drugs.

Adjustment Disorder (Unspecified)

The development of emotional or behavioral symptoms in response to an identifiable stressor(s) occurring within three months of the onset of the stressor(s). These symptoms or behaviors are clinically significant, as evidenced by one or both of the following:

- Marked distress that is out of proportion to the severity or intensity of the stressor, taking into account the context and cultural factors that might influence symptom severity
- Significant impairment in social, occupational, or other important areas of functioning

The DSM-5 lists six different types of adjustment disorders, each with unique signs and symptoms:

- **Adjustment disorder with depressed mood:** feeling sad, tearful, and hopeless
- **Adjustment disorder with anxiety:** feeling nervous and overwhelmed; children may strongly fear being separated from a parent or loved one

- **Adjustment disorder with mixed anxiety and depressed mood:** a combination of depression and anxiety

- **Adjustment disorder with disturbance of conduct:** behavioral problems, such as fighting or skipping school

- **Adjustment disorder with mixed disturbance of emotions and conduct:** a mix of depression, anxiety, and behavioral problems

- **Adjustment disorder unspecified:** symptoms don't fit other types of adjustment disorders but can include problems with family or friends, or school problems

REFERENCE

American Psychiatric Association. (2013). *Diagnostic and Statistical Manual of Mental Disorders* (5th ed.). https://doi.org/10.1176/appi.books.9780890425596

BOYS TOWN RESOURCES

Boys Town National Hotline®
1-800-448-3000
boystown.org/hotline
A crisis, resource, and referral number for kids and parents

Boys Town Behavioral Health Clinics
531-355-3358
boystownpediatrics.org/behavioralhealth
Offers a wide range of services for children who are experiencing behavioral, emotional, academic or substance use concerns.

Boys Town Press books
Resources for counselors, educators, and families

Each main character in this anthology is managing a common yet challenging mental health diagnosis. To learn more about these diagnoses and for tools and resources for children, caregivers, and professionals, be sure to use the accompanying supplemental guides.

978-1-944882-83-9

978-1-944882-84-6

978-1-944882-85-3

A book series and accompanying activity guides focused on childhood friendships, finding your place, advocating for yourself, and being true to who you are.

Jennifer Licate
GRADES 4-8

978-1-944882-63-1   978-1-944882-65-5   978-1-944882-67-9

BoysTownPress.org

For information on Boys Town, its Education Model®, Common Sense Parenting®, and training programs:
boystowntraining.org, boystown.org/parenting
training@BoysTown.org, 1-800-545-5771

For parenting and educational books and other resources:
BoysTownPress.org, btpress@BoysTown.org, 1-800-282-6657